PEGAN DIET
FOR BEGINNERS

Reduce Inflammation, Lose Weight, and Boost Energy with Quick and Easy
Pegan Recipes

Madison Miller

Disclaimer

Copyrights

Disclaimer and Terms of Use

Effort has been made to ensure that the information in this book is accurate and complete. However, the author and the publisher do not warrant the accuracy of the information, text, and graphics contained within the book due to the rapidly changing nature of science, research, known and unknown facts, and internet. The author and the publisher do not hold any responsibility for errors, omissions, or contrary interpretation of the subject matter herein. This book is presented solely for motivational and informational purposes only.

The recipes provided in this collection are for informational purposes only and are not intended to provide dietary advice. A medical practitioner should be consulted before making any changes in diet. Additionally, recipe cooking times may require adjustment depending on age and quality of appliances.

Readers are strongly urged to take all precautions to ensure ingredients are fully cooked in order to avoid the dangers of foodborne illnesses. The recipes and suggestions provided in this book are solely the opinion of the author. The author and publisher do not take any responsibility for any consequences that may result due to following the instructions provided in this book.

Contents

Introduction

The pegan diet the happy union between the paleo and vegan diets. This hybrid diet consists of the best features of both diets. The whole idea of the pegan diet is to reduce the restrictions of both the paleo and the vegan diets while keeping the best elements of each. The result is a better balanced nutrition and a diet that is easier to follow. To understand it better, we will discuss both the origins of the pegan diet, the principles of the paleo and the vegan diets, how both diets can be integrated in one wholesome healthy diet, the pegan diet, the basic guidelines of the pegan diet, the health benefits of following a pegan diet lifestyle, and of course plenty of recipes to get you started.

Let's get started!

Pegan diet: How it all started

The Pegan Diet is a worldwide trending diet owing its spread to its mysterious origin. Its true roots combine certain aspects of two diets - Paleo and Vegan, which don't add up well on paper. The term Pegan was coined by Dr. Mark Hyman, the director of Cleveland Clinic Centre for Functional Medicine, who claims that the Pegan way of eating is not only the most sensible diet designed for the human race, but it is also the healthiest.

To understand the convergence, primary focus has to be laid on the individual aspects involved.

The Vegan Diet

A Vegan diet is built on a certain set of strict rules, with the primary rule prohibiting consumption of all animal products and giving most importance to plant-based foods. This diet lacks meat and other rich sources of bio-molecules like dairy and eggs. Most vegans are extremely careful about what they consume. Apart from the restrictions mentioned above, they also avoid processed animal products like gelatin, which is often added to foods, even those that seem vegan.

The resulting diet is essentially one low in calories, cholesterol, and saturated fat. This can be very advantageous for anyone who wants faster weight loss. It is also be good for those with heart conditions, as it assists in cholesterol and blood pressure regulation. Vegan as a diet is getting increasingly accepted due to its many health benefits.

The Paleo Diet

The paleo Diet has been around for centuries, having originated in The Paleolithic era. Its followers were the ancient people of the Stone Age. As a predecessor, the Paleo diet uses only food available to our ancestors and eliminates or restricts the modern foods. The paleo diet involves higher level consumption of meat and vegetables with a very light sprinkling of fruits and nuts. Additions and alternatives like grains, beans, added sugar, dairy and several kinds of oils are to be avoided.

By way of comparison, the founders of the paleo diet, the cave people, consumed foods that were hunted by our hunter ancestors and included grass-fed meat, fish, eggs, nuts, fruit, and organic low-starch vegetables. Although the fat content isn't restricted, foods like grains, legumes, refined sugar, potatoes, most dairy products, and certain oils are prohibited. On the contrary, a vegan diet is heavily based on plant food consumption. Their diet consists of vegetables, fruits, grains, nuts, and seeds while strictly prohibiting any form of animal product.

Most Paleo dieters have small portions of meat included with every meal. This means that approximately 30-50% of a person's daily energy is obtained through meat. These levels are twice the number when compared to current nutrition guidelines that fluctuate around 15% to 25% of a day's energy obtained through meat.

The vegan diet is very advantageous as it reduces the risk of developing obesity, certain cancers, and type II diabetes. However, the diet falls short of certain amino acids that are the building blocks for proteins, which can only be achieved through diet. Moreover, it is deficient in iron, calcium, zinc, and vitamin B12.

For some individuals, a strict Paleo diet is too heavy and expensive to follow. It is also problematic when you consider the health issues. Veganism, on the other hand, is equally restrictive and quite a challenge for people to stick to. Hence the integration of these two highly opposing diets, the Pegan diet, a perfect mixture of healthy benefits and few limitations makes a lot of sense for those of us who want to follow a healthy lifestyle and agree add a limited amount of animal-based proteins in their diet.   .

The "Pegan" diet

The Pegan diet combines aspects of both the Vegan and Paleo diets while laying most emphasis on the principle of a diet in which you consume wholesome and unprocessed foods. The ultimate goal is to utilize the health benefits associated with the two diets while designing a dietary plan that is flexible and less restrictive.

Designing a dietary plan involves following a certain set of guidelines so we know what to eat and how much. What makes the pegan diet easy to follow is that the rules are so much more adaptable.

Pegan Diet's Guidelines

The previous chapter dealt with how the need for a flexible and healthy diet led to the emergence of pegan diet. As a dietary plan to maintain its properties, even the pegan diet has a certain set of rules and regulations which are to be followed. Unlike other diets, the rules in pegan are user-friendly and can genuinely blend into the needs of a fast-paced life.

What you should be eating

Eat healthy fats

It is important to consume the right kind of fat, which includes coconut; olive; avocado oils as well as nuts and seeds. These fats don't have a high concentration of cholesterol unlike most vegetable oils such as canola, sunflower, corn, and soybean oil. Recent studies have proven that these constitute nearly 10 percent of the day's calorie count.

Eat your plants!

There are several options under this rule contributing to the flexibility. Vegetables and fruits are low in glycemic content. Vegetables and fruits should constitute nearly 75 percent of your diet with two to three vegetable portions per meal. Chose organic deep colored vegetables and fruit and add lots of variety to your diet. This will help in protecting you from utmost diseases because of their high content of phytonutrient.

Treat meat as a Condiment

Meat is an integral component of any diet. A slice of meat is comprised of several vitamins and minerals and is rich in protein. However, it is also rich in saturated fats, the degree by which varies with the variety of meat available. To get the most health benefits out of meat, treat it as a condiment and try eating grass-fed and antibiotic-free meats. Add sparingly small amounts of meat to a meal approximately in the order of a quarter or less of the total ingredients. As hard as it may seem, it is possible. Look for healthier meat, like grass-fed meat, and go lean with poultry or wild caught fish.

Overall, animal protein should make up 25% or less of your nutrition.

Eggs to start the day

Eggs were thought to be unhealthy in decades gone by as they had high levels of cholesterol. However, recent research and food guideline modifications have now decided that it is healthy after all. Eggs have greater concentrations of healthy fats, vitamins, and minerals, apart from being protein rich. Therefore, eating two whole eggs for breakfast won't just fill you up, but also will provide you the necessary nutrients required by your body. Chose organic eggs for a healthier choice.

Eat your low-glycemic grains every day

While grains are entirely banned in the Paleo diet, whole grains have numerous health advantages. Whole grains don't interfere with blood sugar and don't have gluten. Ensure you have half a cup of whole grains like Quinoa, oats, and/or black or wild rice every day.

Half a cup of small-sized beans per day

Beans are very healthy as they are rich in protein, minerals and fiber with several vitamins and minerals. However, if you eat too many beans in a single day, they could cause digestive troubles. This applies for other foods too. You should always eat enough to fill your needs, but avoid overeating as it could lead to serious issues. Half a cup should be an adequate serving. In the various kinds of beans, avoid heavy starch-containing beans, for example, lima beans or kidney beans.

What you should avoid eating

Added refined sugar, processed foods, and gluten

We all know it's bad for you and should be avoided. Research shows that excessive amount of refined sugar as well as processed foods can cause inflammation in the body and several other health issues like weight gain, deregulate the blood glucose levels and disrupt insulin production and many more.

Dairies

Avoid eating heavily in dairy. Lighter foods are recommended. This is because dairies cause lots of digestive problems. Organic goat or sheep dairy products as a treat are fine.

Eliminate soy from your pegan diet

Soy, although a go-to food for the vegan dieters, is eliminated completely from the pegan. Research has shown that soy has can have a disruptive effect on human hormones, especially for woman. It is also agreed that most soy produced in the world have been genetically modified.

Pegan Diet: How Is It Good For You?

Pegan diet is trending worldwide and is spreading to the dietary notebooks of many people who want a flexible diet. The previous chapters dealt with the need for and rules followed under a Pegan diet. This chapter is aimed at determining how it benefits the human body.

The Health Benefits

Low Glycemic Load

Almost all dietary plans try to lower the glycemic load on the human body. Pegan diet successfully lowers and regulates the glycemic levels. Reduction in the levels of sugar, flour, and refined carbohydrates will lower the glycemic content and lowers the risk of developing diabetes.

Boost Energy Levels

One of the best thing of the pegan diet is how energized you will feel after a few days of "clean" eating once you have eliminated refined sugars, processed food, and replaced these unhealthy foods by healthy low toxicity nutritious foods. The feeling sluggishness and heaviness will disappear and be replaced by vital energy and a feeling of well-being.

Essential Vitamins and Nutrients

The Pegan diet is a mosaic of colors with its high fruit and vegetable content, rich in essential vitamins and nutrients including phytonutrients, which serve to aid our immunity against most diseases.

Low Toxicity

The Pegan diet specifically focuses on local, organic, and farm-fresh fruits, vegetables, and meats. This contributes in minimizing the development of toxic levels in our body by eliminating pesticides, antibiotics, and toxic hormones from the diet. The diet also restricts the consumption of genetically modified (GMO) foods to a minimum in an attempt to keep you protected and prone.

Heart Disease Risk Minimized

The diet has consumption of healthy fats like the omega 3 fatty acids that have a positive effect on the whole body. More importantly, they can lower the risk of development of heart diseases. It also has a significant role to play in brain development.

Losing weight and maintaining an ideal weight level

Healthy weight loss is considered to be the most sought-after benefit achieved from following a pegan diet. The concept behind this is quite simple. By eating fewer carbohydrates and eliminating refined sugars, unhealthy fats, and processed and excessively salty foods from our diet, we prevent ourselves from overeating. This causes the sugar cravings to stop, and our insulin level normalizes, making our body more likely to break down fats instead of storing them. Your metabolism improves, and because your intake is healthier and rich in nutrients, you feel full faster and eat less. The diet also makes it easy to maintain your ideal weight as you are fuelling your body with real and nourishing foods.

Reduces inflammation

The healthy food choices of the pegan diet have been proven to reduce inflammation in the body, particularly of the joints and the pain associated with it in diseases such as arthritis. Avoiding added refined sugars, processed foods and limiting the amounts of carbs in the diet helps reduce inflammation.

Pegan Breakfast Recipes

Almond Butter Bread

Serves 2

Ingredients

1¼ cups bananas, mashed

2 eggs

¼ cup almond butter or any other nut butter

2 tablespoons grass fed butter

¼ cup coconut flour

½ tablespoon ground cinnamon

½ teaspoon baking soda

½ teaspoon baking powder

½ teaspoon vanilla

A pinch sea salt

Method

1. Preheat oven at 350°F
2. Blend together bananas, eggs, nut butter, and butter in a blender.
3. Add coconut flour, cinnamon, baking soda, baking powder, vanilla, and salt. Pulse again until well combined.

4. Transfer to a greased bread pan. Spread it all over the pan. Smooth the top with a spatula.

5. Bake in a preheated oven at 350 degrees F for about 45 minutes or until a toothpick comes out clean when inserted in the center.

6. Remove from the oven. Place on a wire rack to cool completely. Slice and serve.

Sweet Potato Hash

Serves 4

Ingredients

2 large sweet potatoes, peeled, shredded

1/8 teaspoon salt

Freshly ground black pepper powder to taste

½ teaspoon garlic powder or to taste

1 teaspoon onion powder

1 teaspoon oregano

¼ cup olive oil

½ teaspoon red pepper flakes (optional)

4 large eggs

1½ tablespoons

Kosher salt to taste

Method

1. Place the sweet potatoes in a large bowl. Add salt, pepper, oregano, garlic, and onion powders. Mix well.

2. Place a large skillet over medium heat. Add 3 tablespoons oil. When the oil heats up, add sweet potatoes. Sauté for a couple of minutes. Cover and cook on a low flame until soft.

3. Meanwhile, place another pan on medium heat. Add 1 tablespoon oil. Crack the eggs into the pan.
4. Sprinkle salt and pepper. Cover and cook until the consistency of the eggs you desire.
5. To serve, divide the hash into 4 individual plates. Gently remove the eggs and place an egg each on top of the hash and serve.

Eggs with Avocado and Salsa

Serves 1

Ingredients

2 large eggs, beaten

½ avocado, sliced

2 tablespoons salsa

¼ cup almonds slivered

Sea salt to taste

Freshly ground black pepper to taste

Cooking spray

Method

1. Place a nonstick skillet over medium heat.
2. Spray with cooking spray.
3. Add the eggs. Cook until the bottom side is done. Flip sides and cook the other side too.
4. Season with salt and pepper. Top with salsa, almonds, and avocado. Serve immediately.

Chia Seed and Black Rice Porridge

Serves 2

Ingredients

½ cup black rice, soaked in water for a minimum of 3 hours

½ can full fat coconut milk + more for serving

2 tablespoons chia seeds

¼ cup water

1/8 teaspoon sea salt

¼ teaspoon vanilla extract

½ tablespoon maple syrup

2 tablespoons unsweetened coconut flakes

½ a passion fruit, cored

A few mango slices

Method

1. Add rice, coconut milk, chia seeds, water, salt, and vanilla extract to a heavy-bottomed saucepan. Place the pan over medium heat. Bring to a boil.

2. Reduce heat and simmer for about 30-35 minutes until cooked. If it is too thick or the rice is not cooked, add more water. Add maple syrup. Stir well and remove from heat and keep aside.

3. Serve in individual bowls. Top with coconut flakes, passion fruit, and mangos.
4. Pour a little coconut milk and serve.

Overnight Banana Blueberry Chia Oats

Serves 2

Ingredients

2 tablespoons chia seeds

1 cup oats

2 cups almond milk

2 bananas, sliced

½ cup blueberries

2 medjool dates, chopped

¼ teaspoon ground cinnamon

¼ cup almonds, chopped

Method

1. Add oats, chia seeds, and almonds to an airtight container. Cover and refrigerate for 7 – 8 hours.
2. Add bananas, blueberries, dates, cinnamon, and almonds. Serve cold or hot.

Thick Almond Butter Banana Smoothie

Serves 2-3

Ingredients

3 frozen bananas, sliced

6 small dates or 3 large dates, pitted

1½ tablespoons smooth almond butter

1½ tablespoons chia seeds

¾ cup hemp milk or almond milk or coconut milk

½ cup water

Method

1. Blend together all the ingredients in a blender until soft.
2. Transfer into glasses. Serve with ice.

Apple Cinnamon Smoothie

Serves 2-3

Ingredients

2 small apples, sliced

1 cup rolled oats

1 teaspoon ground cinnamon

½ teaspoon ground nutmeg

2 tablespoons almond butter

1 cup unsweetened coconut milk

3-4 ice cubes

1 cup cold water

Method

1. Place oats and water in a bowl. Let it soak for about 5 minutes. Transfer to a blender.
2. Add rest of the ingredients, and blend until smooth.
3. Serve with ice, garnished with cinnamon and nutmeg powders.

Tomato Dill Frittata

Serves 2-3

Ingredients

1 teaspoon coconut oil

4 eggs, whisked

2 tomatoes, diced

1 tablespoon fresh dill, chopped

1 tablespoon fresh chives, chopped

2 garlic cloves, minced

½ teaspoon red pepper flakes

Salt to taste

Pepper powder to taste

Method

1. preheated oven at 325°F
2. Grease a small pan with coconut oil.
3. Mix together all the ingredients in a bowl. Pour into the pan.
4. Place the pan in a preheated oven. Bake for about 30 minutes or until set.
5. Garnish with dill and chives and serve.

Easy Breakfast Casserole

Serves 2-3

Ingredients

2 tablespoons coconut oil, melted

1 medium sweet potato or yam, diced

½ teaspoon fine sea salt or to taste

¾ pound breakfast sausage

1 small yellow onion, diced

1 cup chopped spinach

5 eggs, whisked

¼ teaspoon salt

½ teaspoon garlic powder

Method

1. Preheat oven at 400° F
2. Place the sweet potatoes in a bowl. Add salt and coconut oil. Toss. Transfer into a greased baking dish.
3. Bake in preheated oven for about 25 minutes until softened. Remove from the oven.
4. Place a pan over medium heat. Add sausages and onions. Sauté until browned.

5. Transfer into the baking dish. Add spinach, eggs, salt, and garlic powder to the dish. Mix well.

6. Place the dish back in the oven, and bake for about 30 minutes or until set.

Pumpkin Spice Muffins

Serves 2

Ingredients

6 tablespoons coconut flour

¼ cup pumpkin puree

6 tablespoons maple syrup

3 eggs

½ teaspoon ground cinnamon

¼ teaspoon ground ginger

¼ teaspoon ground cloves

¼ teaspoon baking soda

1 teaspoon apple cider vinegar

Method

1. preheated oven at 350°F
2. Add all the ingredients to a bowl, and whisk well until smooth.
3. Grease a muffin tin, or line with parchment paper. Pour the batter into the molds up to ⅔full.
4. Bake in preheated oven for about 25 minutes or until the center is firm.
5. Let it cool about 10 minutes. Cool on a wire rack and serve.

Pegan Lunch Recipes

Vegan Loaded Sweet Potatoes

Serves 4

Ingredients

3 medium sweet potatoes, washed, scrubbed, pricked all over with a fork

1½ cans black beans, drained, rinsed

1½ bunches kale

1½ tablespoons extra virgin olive oil

2 cloves garlic, minced

Salt to taste

Pepper to taste

Vegan Green Goddess dressing (recipe follows)

Method

1. Preheated oven at 375° F
2. Bake the sweet potatoes for about 50-60 minutes or until the potatoes are fork tender but still remain firm. When done, chop the sweet potatoes.

3. Place a saucepan with olive oil over medium heat. Add garlic and sauté until light brown. Add kale and ½ cup water. Mix well. Cover and cook until the kale is done.

4. Add beans and stir well. Cook for 3-4 minutes, and remove from heat. Add salt and pepper and mix.

5. Serve with sweet potatoes and green goddess dressing.

Vegan Green Goddess Dressing

Yields 10 oz.

Ingredients

1 garlic clove, minced
2 small avocadoes, pitted
8 tablespoons cold water, more if needed
2 tablespoons apple cider vinegar*
2 tablespoons fresh lemon juice
¼ cup extra virgin olive oil
1 bunch of fresh basil
¼ cup fresh parsley
6 green onions (scallions)
1 teaspoon sea salt
1 pinch red pepper chili flakes

Method

1. Place all the ingredients in the food processor and mix on low until well mix.
2. Adjust the dressing consistency with by adding cold water, if needed.
3. Place dressing in an airtight container and chill before using.
4. Keep unused dressing in an airtight container up to 4 days.

Note: if like a touch of sweetness in your dressing, add a pitted date to the dressing.

Super Spinach Salad

Serves 2-3

Ingredients

2 cups baby spinach

1 cup purple cabbage, shredded

½ cucumber, sliced

½ Granny Smith apple, peeled, cored and diced

¼ cup onion, sliced

½ cup button mushrooms, sliced

½ cup cooked chicken breast, cubed

1 tablespoon chopped walnuts

Dressing

½ teaspoon garlic powder

½ teaspoon onion powder

3 tablespoons avocado oil

1 tablespoon apple cider vinegar

1 dash honey

1 dash Dijon mustard

Sea salt to taste

Freshly cracked pepper to taste

Method

1. Mix together all the vegetables and the chicken in a large bowl.

2. Whisk together all the dressing ingredients until well combined.

3. Pour the dressing over the salad. Toss well and serve.

Crowd-Pleasing Vegan Caesar Salad

Serves 4

Ingredients

Roasted chickpeas croutons

2 cups chickpeas, drained, rinsed, and pat dried

1 teaspoon extra virgin olive oil

1 teaspoon fine grain sea salt

1 teaspoon garlic powder

Cayenne pepper optional

Dressing

1 cup raw cashews, soaked overnight

½ cup water

4 tablespoons extra virgin olive oil

2 tablespoons lemon juice

1 tablespoon Dijon mustard

1 teaspoon garlic powder

2 small garlic clove

1 tablespoon vegan Worcestershire sauce

4 teaspoons capers

1 teaspoon fine grain sea salt and pepper, or to taste

Nut and seed parmesan cheese

½ cup raw cashews

2 tablespoons raw sesame seeds

4 tablespoons hulled hemp seeds

2 tablespoons extra virgin olive oil

2 tablespoons nutritional yeast

1 teaspoon garlic powder

Fine-grain sea salt, to taste

Greens

1 medium bunch Lacinato kale, de-stemmed, chopped

4 small heads romaine lettuce, chopped

Method

1. Preheat the oven to 400°F.

2. To make the roast chickpea croutons, place the chickpeas in a baking dish. Sprinkle oil and toss well to coat. Sprinkle garlic powder, salt, and cayenne pepper.

3. Roast in oven for 20 minutes. Gently swirl the pan around so the chickpeas roll. Roast for 15-20 minutes more until light golden brown. Cool.

4. To make the dressing, blend together all the ingredients of the dressing until smooth and keep aside.

5. To make the parmesan cheese, add cashews to the food processor, and pulse until the cashews are chopped. Add rest of the ingredients, and blend until smooth.

6. To serve, place the kale and lettuce in a large serving bowl. Add the dressing and serve.

Roasted Garlic and Zucchini Bisque

Serves 4

Ingredients

1¼ pounds zucchini, cut into one inch pieces

1 leek, chopped

1 small yellow onion, chopped

2 cloves of garlic, peeled

1 tablespoon coconut oil, melted

¼ cup raw cashews, soaked for at least 3-4 hours

1¼ cups filtered water

Salt to taste

Pepper to taste

Method

1. Line a cookie sheet with parchment paper. Lay the zucchini, leek, onions, and garlic on it. Sprinkle coconut oil.

2. Bake in a preheated oven at 400°F F for 20 minutes.

3. Cool and blend in a blender with cashews and water until smooth and creamy.

4. Transfer the contents to a heavy bottomed saucepan, and simmer for 5-7 minutes. Add salt and pepper.

5. Serve with extra virgin olive oil.

Lemon Garlic Shrimp over Cauliflower Mash

Serves 4

Ingredients

Lemon Garlic Shrimp

3 cloves garlic, minced

1 slice bacon (optional)

1 tablespoon grass fed butter

1 tablespoon olive oil

¼ cup white wine, or bottled clam juice

¼ sweet onion, thinly sliced

½ teaspoon crushed red pepper flakes, or to taste

¼ teaspoon dried oregano

Juice of one lemon

Kosher salt to taste

Freshly ground black pepper, to taste

1 tablespoon fresh oregano, chopped

Marinade

Zest of ½ lemon, grated

2 cloves garlic, minced

1½ tablespoons extra-virgin olive oil

½ teaspoon dried oregano

½ pound raw shrimp, shelled and de-veined

Cauliflower Mash

1 medium head of cauliflower, cut into large florets

4 cloves garlic, peeled

2 tablespoons extra-virgin olive oil

Kosher salt to taste

Freshly ground black pepper, to taste

¼ cup vegetable broth

Method

1. Mix together all the ingredients of the marinade, place in a zip lock bag, and refrigerate for 2-4 hours.

2. Place the cauliflower and garlic in a baking dish. Sprinkle olive oil, salt, and pepper and toss.

3. Cover the dish with foil, and roast in a preheated oven at 400°F for 15-20 minutes until the vegetables are light brown.

4. Transfer to a food processor, and add a little butter. Pulse, add broth, and pulse again until you get a mash-like consistency. Add salt and pepper and keep warm.

5. Place the bacon in a pan, and cook until crisp and brown. Remove with slotted spoon, and place on paper towels. Crumble when cool.

6. To make lemon garlic shrimp, to the same pan add onions. (Add butter and olive oil only if you are not using bacon). Sauté until translucent, then add garlic, red pepper flakes, and oregano, and sauté until fragrant.

7. Add wine. Cook until the wine reduces in quantity. Add shrimp and cook for not more than 3-4 minutes until shrimp are opaque. Flip shrimp a couple of times. Add lemon juice and remove from heat.

8. Add salt and pepper.

9. To serve, place the cauliflower mash in a serving bowl. Top with shrimp and sauce. Garnish with bacon and fresh parsley.

Vegan Sweet Potato Enchiladas with Avocado Cilantro Cream Sauce

Serves 2

Ingredients

1 cup sweet potato, peeled and chopped, boiled in a pot of water, drained

½ tablespoon olive oil

½ red onion, chopped

2 garlic cloves, minced

Sea salt to taste

Freshly ground pepper

½ red bell pepper, chopped

½ 15-ounce can black beans, rinsed and drained

2 cups enchilada sauce

½ tablespoon fresh lime juice

½ teaspoon chili powder

½ teaspoon ground cumin

½ teaspoon salt

5-6 corn tortillas

Avocado cilantro sauce

¼ cup fresh cilantro

½ medium avocado

1 tablespoon lime juice

⅛ sea salt

½ teaspoon garlic powder

Fresh cilantro leaves, for serving

Sliced green onion, for serving

Method

1. Place a skillet over medium heat. Add oil, onion, and garlic, and sauté until the onions are soft. Add bell pepper, sweet potato, black beans, salt, and pepper. Heat thoroughly.
2. Remove from heat, and add ¼ cup enchilada sauce, lime juice, chili powder and salt.
3. Place this filling in the tortillas and roll it up.
4. Add ½ cup enchilada sauce to a greased baking dish. Place the tortillas with its seam side down in the dish.
5. Pour the remaining enchilada sauce over the tortillas.
6. Bake in a preheated oven at 350°F for about 15-20 minutes.
7. Meanwhile, make the avocado cilantro sauce. Blend together all the ingredients along with a tablespoon or 2 of water until smooth.
8. Serve the enchiladas with this sauce.

Grape, Avocado, and Baby Kale Salad with Quinoa

Serves 4

Ingredients

3 cups baby kale (or baby spinach)

¾ cup cooked quinoa

¼ cup grapes, halved

½ cup beets cut into small cubes

½ cup cucumber, cut into small cubes

½ avocado, cubed

2 tablespoons white balsamic vinegar

Sea salt to taste

Black pepper to taste

Method

1. Mix together all the ingredients well and serve.

Zucchini and Sweet Potato Frittata

Serves 2

Ingredients

1 tablespoon coconut oil

4 eggs, whisked

1 medium sweet potato, peeled, cut in slices

2 sliced zucchinis

½ sliced red bell pepper

1 tablespoon fresh parsley

Salt to taste

Pepper to taste

Method

1. Place a pan with oil over medium heat. Add sweet potatoes and cook until tender.
2. Add zucchini and bell pepper. Sauté for 3-4 minutes.
3. Pour the egg over the vegetables. Season with salt and pepper.
4. Reduce heat and cook until the eggs are set.
5. Place the pan under a preheated broiler and broil until golden brown.
6. Garnish with parsley, cut into wedges and serve.

Bacon, Grape & Broccoli Salad

Serves 2

Ingredients

2 medium heads broccoli, cut into small florets

¾ cup red or green grapes, halved

5 slices bacon

1 small onion, chopped

¼ cup almonds, slivered or chopped

¾ cup paleo mayonnaise

2 tablespoons lemon juice

Method

1. Steam the broccoli in a double boiler until just tender, about 2-4 minutes. Place the broccoli in a strainer and let cold water run over to stop the cooking process. Set aside.

2. Cook the bacon in a pan over medium heat until both the sides are crispy.

3. Place all the ingredients in a large salad bowl. Toss well, and serve.

Raw Zucchini Caponata

Serves 2

Ingredients

2 medium zucchinis, diced

2 medium Roma tomatoes, diced

¼ cup Spanish pitted olives, sliced

2 tablespoons marinated capers

Zest of ½ small lemon, grated

1 green onion, chopped

2 anchovies, finely chopped

Dressing

1 clove garlic, minced

¼ teaspoon salt

1 teaspoon tomato paste

1 tablespoon white or red wine vinegar

2 -3 tablespoons olive oil

½ teaspoon honey or brown rice syrup (optional)

Garnish

2 tablespoons pine nuts, toasted

2 tablespoons grated Parmesan or nutritional yeast (optional)

Method

1. Whisk together all the ingredients of the dressing.

2. Place rest of the ingredients in a large bowl. Pour the dressing, toss well, and serve.

Snacks Recipes

Pecan Pie Balls

Serves 2

Ingredients

2 cups dates, pitted

2 cups pecans

1 teaspoon sea salt

1 teaspoon pure vanilla extract

Method

1. Place all the ingredients in a food processor. Pulse until it forms a dough.

2. Remove and form into small balls. Refrigerate and serve.

Sweet Potato Chips

Serves 2

Ingredients

2 large sweet potatoes, cut into ⅛ inch slices

2 tablespoons olive oil

Salt to taste

Pepper to taste

Method

1. Place the sweet potato slices in a large baking dish.

2. Sprinkle oil, salt, and pepper.

3. Bake in a preheated oven at 400°F for about 25 minutes. Flip sides in between a couple of times.

Spicy Cauliflower

Serves 2

Ingredients

1 head cauliflower, cut into bite-size florets

¼ teaspoon cayenne pepper

½ tablespoon paprika

½ teaspoon red chili pepper flakes

½ teaspoon dried oregano

Pinch of salt and ground black pepper

4 tablespoons coconut oil

Directions

1. Preheat the oven to 375°F.
2. Toss all ingredients in a mixing bowl. Season with salt and pepper.
3. Place on the baking dish in preheated oven.
4. Bake for 15 to 20 minutes until cauliflower is tender.

Garlic Mushroom Quinoa

Serves 2

Ingredients

½ cup quinoa, cooked according to instructions on package

½ tablespoon olive oil

½ pound crimini mushrooms, thinly sliced

3 cloves garlic, minced

½ teaspoon dried thyme

Kosher salt and freshly ground black pepper, to taste

1 tablespoon nutritional yeast (optional)

Method

1. Place a skillet with olive oil over medium heat.
2. Add mushrooms, garlic, and thyme. Sauté until tender.
3. Add salt, pepper, and quinoa. Mix well.
4. Serve garnished with nutritional yeast, if desired.

Spinach, Bacon and egg cupcake

Yields 12 cupcakes

Ingredients

1 tablespoon coconut oil

6 bacon strips, cut each into 2

5 eggs, beaten

1 teaspoon herbs of Provence

Salt and black pepper

3 cups spinach, chopped

Method

1. Pre-heat the oven to 375°F.

2. Grease a 12-hole muffin pan with coconut oil.

3. Line the cups on the inner sides with a bacon piece.

4. Combine eggs with spinach, and herb of Provence in a large bowl. Season with salt and pepper to taste. Mix well.

5. Pour equal amount of the egg mixture into each muffin whole.

6. Bake in oven until the eggs are set, about 25 to 30 minutes.

7. Remove from the oven, and let it cool for a couple of minutes.

8. Loosen the edges with a knife, gently remove, and place on a serving plate. Serve warm.

No-Bake Almond Joy Granola Bars

Serves 2

Ingredients

¼ cup almonds, sliced

½ cup rice crisp cereal cups rolled oats

6 tablespoons rolled oats

2 tablespoons unsweetened shredded coconut

1 tablespoon chia seeds

2 tablespoons coconut oil, melted

¼ cup almond butter

¼ cup coconut nectar syrup

½ teaspoon vanilla extract

A pinch of fine grain sea salt

2 tablespoons non-dairy mini chocolate chips

Method

1. In a large bowl, mix together oats, rice crisp cereal, almonds, coconut and chia seeds.
2. Place a pot over low heat with coconut oil. When melted, remove from heat, and add almond butter, coconut nectar, and vanilla, and mix well until smooth.
3. Pour this mixture over the oats mixture, and mix well adding salt.
4. Line a square pan with 2 parchment papers.

5. Transfer the mixture to the pan, and spread it all over the pan. Smooth with a spatula.
6. Sprinkle chocolate chips, and press the mixture lightly with a pastry roller.
7. Place the pan to the freezer. Freeze for 15-20 minutes.
8. Slice into bars and store in the refrigerator until use.

Tomato Cream Sauce with Zucchini Noodles

Serves 2

Ingredients

½ cup full fat coconut milk

½ cup pizza sauce

¾ tablespoon coconut oil

2¼ teaspoons arrowroot or potato starch

Salt to taste

Pepper powder to taste

2 teaspoon onion powder

1 teaspoon garlic powder

½ teaspoon red pepper flakes to taste

3 zucchinis, made into noodles using a julienne peeler

½ cup baby kale

¼ cup cherry tomatoes, halved

1 tablespoon pine nuts

Method

1. Mix together all the ingredients except noodles, pine nuts and tomatoes in a saucepan. Place the pan on medium heat, and stir constantly until thickened.

2. Add noodles and heat thoroughly. Add more seasonings if necessary.

3. Serve topped with pine nuts and tomatoes.

Spicy Broccoli and Peas Chicken Stir Fry

Serves 4-6

Ingredients

Chicken and marinade

2 small chicken boneless chicken breasts, cubed (about 4 oz. each)

2 tablespoons apple cider vinegar

2 tablespoons of extra-virgin olive oil

1 tablespoon honey

½ teaspoon red pepper chili flakes

1 teaspoon lemon or lime zest

1 teaspoon dry thyme

Stir-fry

3 tablespoons extra virgin olive oil

1 medium onion, diced

2 cloves garlic, minced

1 broccoli, cut into florets

Salt and black pepper to taste

½ teaspoon red chili pepper flakes, or more if you like it very spicy

2 cups fresh shelled peas (can use frozen peas)

2 cup cooked black rice

Method

1. Add the chicken to a Ziploc bag. Pour in the apple cider vinegar, olive oil, honey, chili flakes, zest, and thyme. Seal the bag and make sure the all the ingredients are well combined. Place in the refrigerator and let marinate for 30 minutes to 1 hour.

2. Warm half of the olive oil in a large sauté pan. A wok works well for stir-frying over medium-high heat.

3. Add the onions and sauté for 1 minute. Add in the minced garlic and stir-fry for 1 more minute.

4. Add the marinated chicken cubes with the juice of the left over marinade. Stir-fry for 6-8 minutes, or until the chicken is done. Juice run clear when poked with a fork and internal heat read 165°F on instant meat thermometer. Remove the chicken from pan and set aside

5. Add the remaining oil if needed. Stir-in the broccoli and sauté for 1-2 minutes. Add the peas and the reserved chicken. Stir fry for another 1-2 minutes until all the ingredients are cooked through.

6. Serve in bowls over the cooked black rice.

Skinny Pad Thai with Courgette Noodles

Serves 4

Ingredients

¼ cup coconut aminos

2 tablespoons coconut palm sugar

2 tablespoons lime juice

2 large garlic clove, finely minced

1 teaspoon coconut flour diluted in 2 tablespoons cold water

2 small red chili, finely chopped

2 shallots, finely chopped

1 teaspoon tamarind paste

2 small bunches green onions, finely chopped (scallions)

8 large raw prawns, deveined, cut along the spine

2 large courgettes (zucchini) make into noodles using a julienne peeler or a spiralizer

2 eggs, beaten

2 tablespoons coconut oil

¼ cup crushed cashews to serve

2 tablespoons cilantro, finely chopped

Lime wedges to serve

Method

1. Place coconut aminos, sugar, lime juice, garlic, and tamarind paste in a bowl, and mix until the sugar dissolves

2. Heat a wok with oil in it. Add shallots and spring onions. Sauté for about a minute, add prawns and cook until pink.

3. Add the sauce mix and sauté for a couple of minutes.

4. Move all the ingredients to one side of the wok.

5. Add egg in the middle. When it is slightly set, scramble it, and mix it with rest of the ingredients in the wok.

6. Place the noodles over a serving platter. Top with prawns and sprinkle cashews.

7. Garnish with cilantro and spring onions.

Pegan Dinner Recipes

Sizzling Sausage Skillet

Serves 2

Ingredients

½ pound sausage

½ green bell pepper, sliced

½ red bell pepper, sliced

¼ cup onions, diced

1 sweet potato, diced

1½ tablespoons coconut oil

2 tablespoon coconut oil

1 teaspoon minced garlic

Sea salt and freshly cracked black pepper to taste

Method

1. Place a saucepan over medium-high heat. Add 1 tablespoon coconut oil. When oil is heated, add garlic, and sweet potatoes, and sauté until brown on the edges, about 10 minutes.

2. Meanwhile, place a nonstick skillet over medium heat. Add the sausage, and cook until browned. Remove and slice into 1-inch thick chunks.

3. Add the sausages to the saucepan containing sweet potatoes along with onions. Cook for an additional 2-4 minutes, stirring in between a couple of times until the onions become fragrant and potatoes are fork tender.

4. Add the remaining coconut oil to the nonstick skillet. Add the peppers and sauté for a while until crisp. Transfer to the saucepan containing the sweet potatoes mixture. Mix well. Remove from heat.

5. Serve sprinkled with salt and pepper if desired.

Spiced Lentil Soup with Coconut Milk

Serves 2-3

Ingredients

¾ cup green lentils, rinsed, soaked in water for 5-6 hours, and then drained

3 cups vegetable broth

½ teaspoon turmeric

1 teaspoon curry powder

1 teaspoon dried thyme

½ tablespoon coconut oil

1 medium yellow onion, diced

1 stalk lemon grass (remove the outer layer), minced

½ teaspoon sea salt or to taste

¼ teaspoon ground cardamom

¼ teaspoon ground cinnamon

A pinch of red pepper flakes

A pinch nutmeg, grated

¾ cup full fat coconut milk

1 ½ tablespoons lemon juice

1 cup baby spinach

½ cup coconut flakes, toasted

Cilantro leaves to garnish

Method

1. To a large pot, add lentils, broth, thyme, turmeric powder, and curry powder. Bring to a boil.

2. Lower the heat and simmer for about 20-25 minutes.

3. Meanwhile, heat a pan with coconut oil in it. Add onions and sauté until brown. Add rest of the ingredients except lemon juice, and sauté for a minute. Transfer the entire contents to the pot.

4. Simmer until the lentils are cooked.

5. Add coconut milk and spinach, and simmer for 4-5 minutes. Taste and adjust the seasoning. Add lemon juice.

6. Ladle into bowls. Garnish with toasted coconut flakes and cilantro.

Skinny Shrimp Scampi with Zucchini Noodles

Serves 2

Ingredients

1 tablespoon olive oil

½ pound jumbo shrimp, shelled, deveined

½ tablespoon garlic, minced

¼ teaspoon crushed red pepper flakes

2 tablespoons white wine

1 tablespoon lemon juice

1 medium zucchini

2 tablespoons fresh parsley, chopped

Method

1. Make noodles of the zucchini with a spiralizer or julienne peeler.

2. Place a skillet over medium-low heat. Add olive oil. When oil is heated, add garlic and sauté for a minute. Add red pepper flakes and stir for a few seconds.

3. Add shrimp. Cook for 3-4 minutes until the shrimp are cooked through.

4. Sprinkle salt and pepper. Use a slotted spoon, and place the shrimp in a bowl.

5. Raise the heat to medium. Add white wine and lemon juice. Scrape any browned bits from the base of the pan. Cook for a couple of minutes.

6. Add zucchini noodles, and cook for a couple of minutes. Add the shrimp back to the pan. Add salt and pepper to taste. Mix well.

7. Garnish with parsley, and serve immediately.

Garlic & Saffron Oil Poached Prawns, Warm Zucchini, Roasted Tomatoes

Serves 2

Ingredients

6 fresh king prawns, peeled, deveined, leave the tails on

¾ cup mild extra virgin olive oil

4 garlic cloves, peeled, halved

A few threads of saffron

1 medium zucchini, peeled into ribbons using a peeler

½ red chili

Juice of ½ lemon

Zest of ½ lemon, grated

½ tablespoon fresh parsley, chopped

1 vine of cherry tomatoes (about 8-10 tomatoes)

1 tablespoon balsamic vinegar

Sea salt to taste

Black pepper to taste

Method

1. Place a saucepan over medium heat. Add oil. When the oil is heated to about 180° F, remove from the heat. Add garlic, saffron and a pinch of salt. Stir well.

2. Keep aside to cool for about 30-40 minutes.

3. Preheat the oven to 350°F

4. Place the cherry tomatoes along with the vine on a baking sheet. Sprinkle a little olive oil over the tomatoes.

5. Place the baking sheet in oven for about 30 minutes.

6. Remove the baking sheet, and sprinkle balsamic vinegar over the tomatoes. Place the baking sheet back in the oven and roast for 10 more minutes.

7. To make poached prawns, place the saucepan with oil back on heat. When the temperature reaches about 175°F, add the prawns and remove from heat.

8. After a few minutes turn the prawns around. In case the oil has cooled, reheat the oil up to 165°F. The prawns will become harder, and pink in color. Leave it in the oil for a while.

9. Place a frying pan over medium heat. Add about a tablespoon of the oil from the pan to the frying pan. Add chilies, zucchini, and lemon zest. Sauté for about 1-2 minutes. Transfer into a serving bowl.

10. Add salt, pepper, and a little extra virgin olive oil. Add the roasted tomatoes. Strain the prawns and garlic, and place on the tomatoes and serve.

Show-off Paleo Lasagna

Serves 2

Ingredients

Beef and tomato sauce

1 medium brown onion finely cut

1 tablespoon virgin olive oil

½ pound grass-fed beef, minced

¾ teaspoon sea salt

½ teaspoon ghee

1/3 cup red wine

2 garlic cloves, minced

1/3 teaspoon freshly ground black pepper

1/3 teaspoon sweet paprika

1 ½ cups fresh tomato puree

Lasagna layer

1 medium parsnip, peeled, thinly sliced

1 medium eggplant, sliced into 1/2 inch-thick rounds

½ teaspoon sea salt

6 tablespoons virgin olive oil

1 teaspoon ghee

¼ cup torn fresh basil leaves

3 button mushrooms, sliced

1 cup baby spinach leaves

3 small zucchini, sliced vertically into thin ribbons

Cherry tomatoes to garnish

Method

1. Grease a lasagna pan with ghee. Lay parsnip slices at the bottom. Bake in a preheated oven at 350°F for about 15 minutes. Remove from the oven and keep aside.

2. To make beef and tomato sauce, place a saucepan over medium heat. Add 1 tablespoon olive oil. When the oil is hot, add onions and sauté for 3-4 minutes. Add a dash of salt, and sauté until the onions are light brown. Add ghee, and raise the heat to high. Add beef. Break the beef into small pieces, and cook until browned.

3. Add rest of the ingredients of the sauce and mix well. Bring to a boil. Reduce heat and simmer for about 10 minutes.

4. In the meantime, season the eggplant with salt and keep aside in a colander for about 10-15 minutes. Rinse and pat dry with paper towels.

5. Place a frying pan over medium heat. Add a tablespoon of olive oil and a teaspoon of ghee. Add the eggplant in batches, and cook until golden brown on both the sides.

6. Add more oil and ghee if necessary.

7. Preheat the oven to 350°F and place oven rack in the middle position.

8. To layer the lasagna, first place at the bottom the cooked parsnips, add ⅓ of the sauce. Spread it all over. Layer with eggplants followed by basil and mushrooms.

9. Pour rest of the beef sauce. Spread evenly and press down slightly.

10. Layer the spinach followed by zucchini. Sprinkle some olive oil and pepper.

11. Bake in the oven for 30-40 minutes.

Spinach Salad with Nectarines and Pecans

Serves 2

Ingredients

1 avocado, peeled, chopped into chunks

4 cups of baby spinach leaves

1 ripe nectarine, pitted and chopped

1 cup cherry tomatoes, halved

⅔ cup raw pecans, chopped

12-ounce fresh wild salmon with skin or fish of your choice

2 teaspoon avocado oil

1½ tablespoons fresh lemon juice

2 tablespoons walnut oil

½ teaspoons paleo Dijon mustard

Fresh ground black pepper to taste

Method

1. Preheat the oven to 400°F
2. Place a cast iron pan over medium high heat. When the pan is very hot, add avocado oil.
3. Place the salmon in the pan, skin side down at the bottom of the pan. Cook for 2 to 3 minutes.

4. Place the pan in the oven for about 5 minutes or until done.

5. Add lemon juice, mustard, salt and pepper to a bowl. Whisk well. Gently drizzle the walnut oil, whisking simultaneously until thick.

6. Mix together in a large bowl, spinach, nectarines, avocados, tomatoes, and pecans.

7. Pour the dressing on top. Toss well. Finally place the salmon on the top and serve.

Lemon Quinoa Cilantro, Chickpea Salad

Serves 2-3

Ingredients

1 cup dry quinoa

4 cups vegetable broth

Salad

2 cans garbanzo beans, drained, rinsed

2 cups cherry tomatoes, halved

4 avocados, diced

4 cups baby spinach, chopped

1 cup cilantro, chopped

1 onion, chopped

4 cloves garlic, minced

Dressing

1½ tablespoons Dijon mustard

1½ tablespoons olive oil

2 teaspoons agave nectar

1 teaspoon ground cumin

Salt to taste

Pepper powder to taste

Method

1. Place the quinoa and vegetable broth in a pot for about 15 minutes.

2. Place the pot on medium high heat. Bring to a boil.

3. Lower heat to medium-low. Cover and let simmer until the broth is almost dried up, but not completely dried up. Make sure to stir on and off.

4. Uncover, and put aside to cool.

5. To make the dressing, add all the ingredients to a small bowl. Whisk well.

6. Mix together all the ingredients of the salad in a large bowl.

7. Add chickpeas and the cooled quinoa. Mix well.

8. Pour the dressing over the salad. Toss well and serve.

Roasted Vegetable Salad with Garlic Dressing

Serves 4

Ingredients

1 head garlic

3 tablespoons extra virgin olive oil

Sea salt to taste

Ground black pepper to taste

3 large carrots, scrubbed, chopped into chunks, blanched

3 beets, peeled, chopped into chunks, blanched

Greens of the beets, chopped

1 bunch chard

2 tablespoons lemon juice

4 tablespoons of extra virgin olive oil

½ cup raw pepitas, hulled , toasted with a teaspoon of olive oil in a pan

Salt and pepper

Method

1. Preheat the oven to 350°F
2. Place the garlic head on a foil. Add a teaspoon olive oil and salt. Wrap the garlic with foil.
3. Place the garlic wrapped in foil in a baking dish.

4. Bake in the oven for about 15 minutes. Keep aside to cool.

5. Place the carrots on a baking sheet and the beets on another baking sheet. Sprinkle a little olive oil on both and salt.

6. Place both baking sheets in a preheated oven at 400°F, and bake for about 20 minutes.

7. After about 10 minutes, flip the vegetables. When done, remove from the oven, and put aside.

8. Place the chard and beet greens on another baking sheet. Brush with a little olive oil. Bake for 5-6 minutes or until the greens have wilted.

9. To make the dressing, peel the garlic and place in a bowl. Mash the garlic. Add lemon juice and salt and whisk well. Gently pour olive oil, whisking simultaneously until it chickens.

10. Place the carrots and beets in a bowl. Pour half the dressing over it. Toss well.

11. Place the greens on a serving plate. Place the carrots and beets over the greens.

12. Pour rest of the dressing. Sprinkle the pepitas, and season to taste with salt and pepper.

Curried Coconut Quinoa and Greens with Roasted Cauliflower

Serves 2-3

Ingredients

Roasted cauliflower

½ head cauliflower, cut into bite-sized florets

1 tablespoon melted coconut oil or olive oil

¼ teaspoon cayenne pepper

Sea salt to taste

Curried coconut quinoa with greens

1 teaspoon melted coconut oil or olive oil

1 small yellow onion, chopped

½ teaspoon ground ginger

½ teaspoon ground turmeric

½ teaspoon curry powder

¼ teaspoon ground cardamom

½ a 14-ounce can light coconut milk

¼ cup water

½ cup quinoa, rinsed, drained in a fine mesh colander

3 tablespoons raisins

½ teaspoon sea salt

½ tablespoon cider vinegar

2 cups baby arugula or chopped chard or spinach

For garnishing

1 green onion, chopped

A large pinch red pepper flakes

Method

1. Preheat the oven to 425°F.

2. To roast the cauliflower, place the cauliflower in a bowl. Add coconut oil, cayenne pepper, and salt. Toss well, and transfer on to a baking sheet. Roast in oven at 425°F for about 30 minutes or until golden brown. Turn the florets in between a couple of times.

3. To make the curried quinoa, place a heavy bottomed saucepan over medium heat. Add coconut oil and onions. Sauté until the onions are translucent.

4. Add ginger, turmeric, curry powder, and cardamom. Sauté for a few more seconds and add coconut milk, water, quinoa, and raisins. Bring to a boil.

5. Lower heat. Cover and cook for about 15 minutes. Keep aside.

6. After about 5-7 minutes, using a fork, loosen the quinoa. Add greens, salt and vinegar. Stir well.

7. Divide the quinoa into individual serving bowls. Place the roasted cauliflowers on top of the quinoa.

Layered Raw Taco Salad

Serves 2-3

Ingredients

Taco layer

1 cup walnuts, soaked for 5-8 hours

1½ teaspoons chili powder

1 cumin powder

Sea salt to taste

Cayenne pepper, to taste (optional)

Cashew or macadamia cream

2 cups macadamia (or cashew) nuts, soaked in water for

5 -8 hours, drained

1 cup water or more if needed

¼ cup fresh lemon juice or to taste

Sea salt, to taste

Guacamole

2 avocados, preferably ripe, skinned, pitted and chopped
into chunks

½ cup chopped onion

3 tablespoons fresh lime juice

1 tomato, chopped

½ teaspoon garlic powder

½ teaspoon sea salt, or to taste

Other salad ingredients
1 cup lettuce
1 cup baby spinach or any greens of your choice
¼ cup salsa
2 green onions, chopped
Crackers, if desired

Method

1. To make the taco layer, add all the ingredients to a food processor, and pulse until the walnuts are roughly chopped. Transfer into a bowl and keep aside.

2. To make the cashew cream, add all the ingredients to a food processor, and blend until smooth. Add water according to the consistency you desire.

3. To make the guacamole, place the avocado chunks in a bowl. Mash roughly so that a few pieces are visible. Add tomatoes, onions, lime juice, salt, and cumin.

4. To arrange the salad, take an individual serving bowl. Divide and place the greens. Spread little guacamole.

5. Spread the salsa followed by the taco layer.

6. Spread the cashew cream.

7. Garnish with crackers, if desired and green onions and serve.

Kale, Black Bean and Avocado Burrito Bowl

Serves 2

Ingredients
½ cup brown rice, cooked according to instructions on the package
1/8 teaspoon salt

Kale salad
½ bunch curly kale leaves, chopped into bite sized pieces
2 tablespoons lime juice
1 tablespoon olive oil
½ jalapeno, seeded, finely chopped
¼ teaspoon cumin
⅛ teaspoon salt

Avocado salsa verde
½ avocado, pitted, chopped into chunks
¼ cup mild salsa Verde
¼ cup fresh cilantro, chopped
Juice of ½ a lime

Black beans

2 cups black beans, rinsed, drained

¼ cup onions, finely chopped

2 cloves garlic, minced

Chili powder to taste

¼ teaspoon cayenne pepper

Garnish

A few cherry tomatoes cut into thin round slices

A drizzle of hot sauce

Method

1. Fluff the cooked rice with a fork. Add salt and mix well.

2. To make the kale salad, to a large bowl, add all the ingredients of the kale salad. Toss well and keep aside.

3. To make the avocado salsa verde, blend together all the ingredients in a blender until smooth.

4. For black beans, place a skillet over medium heat. Add olive oil. When oil heats up, add onions and garlic. Sauté until the onions are translucent. Add rest of the ingredients and simmer for about 5 minutes. If the mixture is too dry, add a little water.

5. To serve, divide the rice into individual serving bowls. Divide black beans and spread over the rice.
6. Layer the kale salad. Top with the avocado salsa verde.
7. Garnish with cherry tomatoes and hot sauce.

Spicy Thai Style Cashew Sauce with Rice and Roasted Sweet Potatoes

Serves 2

Ingredients

Spicy Thai cashew sauce

¼ cup raw cashew butter

2 tablespoons coconut aminos

1½ tablespoons apple cider vinegar

1 tablespoon honey or agave nectar

½ teaspoon grated fresh ginger

2 cloves garlic, pressed

¼ teaspoon red pepper flakes

1 tablespoon water

Roasted vegetables

1 sweet potato peeled, chopped into 1 inch cubes

½ red bell pepper, cored, deseeded, and sliced into thin strips

1 tablespoons coconut oil (or olive oil)

¼ teaspoon cumin powder

Sea salt, to taste

Rice and garnishes

¾ cup black rice, cooked according to instructions on the package

2 green onions, sliced (green and white parts)

2 tablespoons fresh cilantro, chopped,

¼ cup roasted cashew, crushed

Sriracha sauce (optional)

Method

1. Preheat the oven to 425°F
2. Lay the sweet potatoes on a greased baking sheet. Add coconut oil, cumin, and salt. Toss well. Place on the middle rack of the oven.
3. Lay the bell pepper on another baking sheet, and place on the top rack of the oven.
4. Roast for about 35-40 minutes. Turn the sweet potatoes after about 20 minutes, and remove the bell peppers from the oven.
5. Fluff the cooked rice with a fork and salt.
6. To make the sauce, whisk together all the ingredients of the sauce. Thin the sauce with water to suit your taste.
7. To serve place rice in individual bowls. Place the roasted sweet potatoes and bell peppers over the rice. Pour some sauce. Garnish with green onions, cilantro and cashews.

Seven Vegetable Couscous

Serves 4

Ingredients

Vegetable stew

4 cloves garlic, smashed

3 small turnips, peeled, quartered

2 medium yellow onion, quartered lengthwise, root end intact

2 medium carrots, peeled, cut into 2-inch chunks

1 bulb of fennel, sliced lengthwise with the root ends intact

¼ cup raisins

1½ tablespoons, fresh ginger, peeled, chopped

1 tablespoon kosher salt or to taste

1 teaspoon ground cumin

1 teaspoon paprika

1 teaspoon sugar

1 teaspoon ground turmeric

¼ teaspoon ground cloves

1 cinnamon stick, chopped in half

3 cups water

1½ pound butternut squash, seeded, chopped into wedges

1 medium zucchini, cut into 2-inch rounds

½ 15½ ounce can chickpeas, rinsed, drained

6 sprigs parsley, tied together with a string

½ cup canned whole peeled tomatoes, with juices

3 cups water

Couscous

2 tablespoons grass fed butter or olive oil

Kosher salt and freshly cracked black pepper

½ cauliflower, cut into florets

¼ cup toasted sliced almonds

Harissa sauce for serving

Method

1. Add all the ingredients of the stew to a large pot. Cover with a lid and place the pot over high heat. Bring to a boil.

2. Lower heat and simmer until the vegetables are tender. Discard the cinnamon.

3. To make couscous, place the cauliflower florets in a food processor. Pulse until the cauliflower reaches the size of couscous grains. You can also use a fine grater. Warm the butter or olive oil over medium heat in a large saucepan. Add the cauliflower and sauté for 2-3 minutes until just tender. Season with salt and pepper to taste. Remove from heat. Keep aside for 5 minutes. Transfer to a large serving platter.

4. Remove the vegetables from the stew with a slotted spoon, and place over the cauliflower couscous. Pour a little of the broth too. Garnish with almonds, and serve with Harissa and more broth if necessary.

Super food Crunch Salad with Homemade Balsamic Apple Vinaigrette

Serves 4

Ingredients

Dressing

1 tablespoon extra-virgin olive oil

½ tablespoon apple cider vinegar

½ tablespoon balsamic vinegar

½ teaspoon pure maple syrup, or to taste

½ teaspoon Dijon mustard

1 garlic clove, minced

¼ teaspoon fine grain sea salt

Freshly ground black pepper, to taste

Salad

4 - 5 cups kale, remove stems, shredded

½ pear, thinly sliced, chopped

¼ cup pomegranate arils

2 tablespoons Pepita seeds

2 tablespoons large coconut flakes

1 tablespoon hemp hearts (shelled hemp seeds)

1 teaspoon black sesame seeds (optional)

A generous pinch cinnamon

Method

1. Whisk together all the ingredients of the dressing in a bowl.

2. Add all the ingredients of the salad to a large bowl. Pour dressing. Toss and serve.

Desserts Recipes

Sweet 'n' Salty Chia pudding

Serves 2

Ingredients

6 tablespoons chia seeds

¾ cup unsweetened almond milk

¼ cup pure maple syrup

2 heaped tablespoons cashew butter,

¼ teaspoon salt

6 dates, pitted, chopped

Method

1. Place all the ingredients in a bowl. Whisk well. Refrigerate for a few hours

2. Serve chilled.

Banana Cream Pie Blizzards

Serves 4

Ingredients

2 cups raw cashews, soaked for 6 hours, drained

2 cups unsweetened almond or coconut milk

2 teaspoons pure vanilla extract

10-12 medjool dates, pitted, if dry, soak in hot water for 10 minutes, drain

¼ cup banana powder (ground banana chips)

¼ cup coconut oil, melted

2 bananas, sliced

A few vegan cookies, crushed

Method

1. Blend together all the ingredients except ripe banana to a smooth and creamy puree. Transfer the contents to an ice cream bowl and freeze until done.
2. Serve ice cream with sliced bananas.

No-bake Caramel Chocolate Slice

Serves 4-5

Ingredients

Fudge

2 cups cashews, soaked in hot water for 10 minutes

25 Medjool dates, pitted, soaked in hot water for 10 minutes

¼ cup coconut oil, melted

2 teaspoons raw cacao powder

2 teaspoons vanilla extract or essence

Pinch of salt

¾ cup almond flakes, toasted

Chocolate layer

½ cup coconut oil

¼ cup raw cacao powder

2 tablespoons maple syrup

¼ cup coconut milk

2 teaspoons vanilla extract

Method

1. Blend together all the fudge ingredients except half the almond flakes to a sticky fudge mixture in a large mixing bowl. Transfer the fudge into a square tin lined with parchment paper. Smooth with a spatula. Refrigerate for an hour to chill.

2. Meanwhile, place all the chocolate layer ingredients except the raw cocoa powder in a double boiler. When it is well blended, add cocoa powder and whisk well until smooth. Remove from heat.

3. Pour the chocolate sauce over the fudge. Smooth the top with a spatula. Sprinkle the remaining almond flakes. Refrigerate for 4-5 hours before serving.

Quick Coconut & Chia seed Pudding

Serves 4

Ingredients

½ cup unsweetened coconut, shredded

½ cup chia seeds

1½ cups full fat coconut milk

1 cup coconut water

2 teaspoons vanilla extract

½ teaspoon Himalayan pink salt or to taste

1 cup fresh raspberries

Method

1. Mix together all the ingredients except raspberries in a bowl.
2. Refrigerate for 3-4 hours.
3. Serve with raspberries.

Three-layer, Nut-Free Dream Cups

Serves 2-3

Ingredients

Bottom layer

6 tablespoons melted coconut butter

Middle layer

½ cup sunflower seed butter

3 tablespoons pure maple syrup

¼ cup virgin coconut oil, softened

1 teaspoon vanilla extract

A pinch of fine sea salt

Top layer

½ cup virgin coconut oil, melted

½ cup unsweetened cocoa powder

¼ cup maple syrup

A pinch of fine sea salt

6 tablespoons unsweetened large flake coconut

Method

1. Line a 12 muffin pan with paper liners. Add about a teaspoon of melted coconut butter to each of the mold. Freeze the molds.

2. To make the middle layer, mix together all the ingredients. Add a tablespoon of the filling to each of the frozen molds. Freeze again.

3. To make the top layer, whisk together all the ingredients except large flake coconut. Add a tablespoon of the filling to each of the frozen molds. Finally, add a teaspoon of large flake coconut. Freeze again until set and serve.

Conclusion

If you're looking for an ethical, holistic way of eating then you've found it with the Pegan diet. The principles of the Paleo diet mean you are eating fresh food from the land while Veganism encourages the same thing minus the animal protein.

Peganism allows you to enjoy delicious, satisfying whole foods while still allowing for a little ethically-raised meat protein, low-glycemic grains and legumes on the side. The wide range of foods allowed on the Pegan diet make it a functional lifestyle choice that you can stick to without ever feeling deprived.

Eating the Pegan way means you'll be feeling happy, energetic, and most importantly, you'll feel really great about the fantastic choices you are making.

Other books from Madison Miller

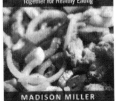

Appendix

Cooking Conversion Charts

1. Volumes

US Fluid Oz.	US	US Dry Oz.	Metric Liquid ml
¼ oz.	2 tsp.	1 oz.	10 ml.
½ oz.	1 Tbsp.	2 oz.	15 ml.
1 oz.	2 Tbsp.	3 oz.	30 ml.
2 oz.	¼ cup	3½ oz.	60 ml.
4 oz.	½ cup	4 oz.	125 ml.
6 oz.	¾ cup	6 oz.	175 ml.
8 oz.	1 cup	8 oz.	250 ml.

Tsp.= teaspoon - Tbsp.= tablespoon – oz.= ounce – ml.= millimeter

2. Oven Temperatures

Celsius (ºC)*	Fahrenheit (ºF)
90	220
110	225
120	250
140	275
150	300
160	325
180	350
190	375
200	400
215	425
230	450
250	475
260	500

*Rounded figures